Riddles For Kids Age 9-12

*300 Funny Riddles and Brain Teasers
for Smart Kids to Enjoy With
the Whole Family*

By Merry Young

Table of Contents

INTRODUCTION

Puzzles, puzzles, everywhere! They're things we love to love and sometimes hate to love, but we always love them. Do you agree with me? A wise man once said that it is good to exercise our brains and wonder about things.

Read and explore all the many different riddles about all the many different things in the world today! Riddles about love; riddles about money; riddles about people and animals. Can you find the answers? There is only one way to find out: start scrolling through this book and explore all of the unanswered truths. Don't worry, I'll be here to help you along your way.
If you can't find the solution to a question, then I'll tell you where the answer is – or even better, I will show you.

Hold on to your seats, boys and girls, because I'm about to share with you some of the world's most priceless pearls. These riddles contained in this book are very special to me and I hope they will be to you too. Some are a little easy; others are obnoxiously difficult; there are a few with a sense of humour; and some odd ones that might scare you a little bit. But I promise you that there is not one riddle that is impossible, because they can all be answered. So, put on your thinking caps and start reading.

"There are a whole lot of things

in this world of ours you haven't even

started wondering about yet."

Roald Dahl, James and the Giant Peach

CUSHY RIDDLES

Love and Family

When you think of your mom and dad kissing, I'm sure it sends a shiver down your spine (As it does if to mine). But to love can be showed in many ways – a kiss, a hug, a friendly wave. Here are some loving riddles for you: see if you can pick up on my clues.

"It doesn't matter who you are or what you look like so long as somebody loves you."

Roald Dahl, the Witches

1. I hurt the most when lost, yet also when not had at all. I'm sometimes the hardest to express, but the easiest to ignore. I can be given to many, or just one.
    What am I?

2. What flowers can be kissed?

3. What is the name for two birds that are in love?

4. After a train crashed, every single person died. Who survived?

5. At the sound of me, men may dream or stomp their feet, women may laugh or sometimes weep. What am I?

6. David's parents have three sons: Snap, Crackle and...?

   (Think carefully on this one: it fooled me!)

7. What did the valentine card say to the stamp?

8.   A doctor and a bus driver are both in love with the same woman, an attractive girl named Sarah. The bus driver had to go on a long bus trip that would last a week (seven days long). Before he left, he gave Sarah seven apples. Why?

9.   Why does love need sunglasses and a cane?

10.   It is not in your tummy but somewhere above. It is thought by many to be the symbol of love.

Animals and Things

That's enough about love, don't you think? Time to move on to things that bark and oink. My favourite animal lives under the seas, but I also love the ones that live in the trees. What are some of the animals that you love most? And I'm not talking about the ones you like in a roast. Figure out my riddles about animal stuff – only if you think you're smart enough.

> *"Fern was up at daylight, trying to rid the world of injustice. As a result, she now has a pig. A small one to be sure, but nevertheless a pig. It just shows what can happen if a person gets out of hed promptly."*
>
> E.B. White, *Charlotte's Web*

1. There's lots of me at Thanksgiving
   But you don't want me to be wasted
   Because my meat's really juicy
   Just so long as I have been basted
   What am I?

2. In a pond, there are three flowers. How many bees are there if both the following statements are true: 1. If each bee lands on a flower, one bee doesn't get a flower. 2. If two bees share each flower, there is one flower left out.

3. How can a leopard change its spots?

4. My wings are used as flippers
    So in water I can flow
    Sometimes when on land I slide
    On my belly in the snow
    What am I?

5. Why are ghosts bad liars?

6. If a brother, his sister, and their dog weren't under an umbrella, why didn't they get wet?

7. I have no sword, I have no spear, yet rule a horde which many fear, my soldiers fight with wicked sting, I rule with might, yet am no king. What am I?

8. I'm a pet that has four legs

   And a tail at the end

   You might hear me barking

   And I'm known as man's best friend

   What am I?

9. Why do turkeys get full on Thanksgiving?

10. Can you guess what animal I am?

    Oh, how I love my dancing feet!

They stay together - oh so neat.

And when I want to walk a line,

They all stay together and do double time.

I count them up, ten times or more,

And race on-off, across the floor.

11. Imagine this: A swarm of bees are going to attack you. You are running as fast as you can, running for your dear life. They are closing in about to sting. How can you escape from them?

12. A duck walked into a bar and watched a stand-up comedian. The duck couldn't stop laughing, but managed to say one thing to the comedian between chuckles. What did the duck say?

13. I have a cape but I'm not a superhero, I have a comb but never use it for my hair, and I am known to be quite territorial. What am I?

14. A sick bird walked into a hospital. What did it ask for from the doctor?

15. Most of the time I am big, scary and hairy and can strike terror in those that I go after. Yet I have one form in which I am colourful, small and kids love to gobble me up. What am I?

16. Who spends the day at the window, goes to the table for meals and hides at night?

17. I live in my little house all alone. There are no windows or doors, and if I want to go out, I have to break through the wall. What am I?

18. What's black and white and blue?

19. If two snakes marry, what will their towels say?

20. What do you get if you cross a hen with a guitar?

Math Riddles

One plus two is three; it's as simple as can be! Or is it? I'm afraid it can be tricky at times, but let's start out a little easy. Just try figure these out, one at a time. I promise you will be fine. If you can't find the answer then I'll give it to you but see how many *you* can do.

"Reading is to the mind what
exercise is to the body."
Richard Steele

1. If a rooster laid 13 eggs and the farmer took eight of them and then another rooster laid 12 eggs and four of them were rotten, how many of the eggs were left?
    Careful with this one – it's tricky!

2. Why is six afraid of seven?

3. Joe bought a bag of oranges on Monday, and ate a third of them. On Tuesday he ate half of the remaining oranges. On Wednesday he looked in the bag to find that he only had two oranges left. How many oranges were originally in the bag?

4. Tara has $30.00 dollars. She bought 5 colouring books that cost $3.00 each, 4 boxes of Crayola crayons that cost $2.00 each. She spends the rest of her money on markers. How much money did she spend on markers?

5. There is a basket containing 5 apples, how do you divide the apples among 5 children so that each child has 1 apple while 1 apple remains in the basket?

6. Tom was on the way to the Park. He met a guy with 7 wives and each of them came with 7 sacks. All these sacks contain 7 cats and each of these 7 cats had 7 kittens. So, in total, how many were going to the Park?

7. There are a certain number of books on my bookshelf. I took a book which is 6th from the right and 4th from the left. Can you find out the number of books on my shelf?

8. Two aeroplanes started the voyage. One flight is flying from London to KL at a speed of 400 MPH. The other flight is flying from KL to London at a speed of 600 MPH. Both these flights met at a point. Which of these flights will be closer to KL?

9. Mary has 7 daughters and each of them has a brother. Can you figure out the total number of kids Mary has?

10. Two hens can lay two eggs in two minutes. If this is the maximum speed possible, what is the total number of hens needed to get 500 eggs in 500 minutes?

11. A taxi driver was called to take a group of passengers to the train station. The station is normally an hour away, but with traffic being extra heavy, it took a full hour and a half. On the return trip the traffic was still as heavy but it took only 90 minutes. Why?

12. A bottle and a cork together cost $1.10. The bottle costs $1.00 more than the cork. How much does the cork cost?

13. You must buy hundred eggs with hundred cents. There are three types of eggs; and you will need to buy all three types. (Goose eggs must be bought in multiples of 20.)

    a. 1 Chicken egg cost 5 cents
    b. 1 Duck egg cost 1 cent
    c. 20 Goose eggs cost 1 cent

    How many chicken, duck and goose eggs do you need to buy?

14. When Tom was 2 years old his sister was half his age. Now, Tom is 100 years old. Then how old is his sister?

15. In a cookie jar, there are ten butter cookies and ten chocolate-chip cookies. Tom sneaks over to the cookie jar in the middle of the night and tries to figure out:

    a. How many cookies do I need to take out of the jar if I want to make sure to get at least two of each kind?

    b. How many cookies do I need to take out of the jar if I want to make sure to get at least two butter cookies?

Word Riddles

Sometimes I can be confusing in what I say. My job is to try and trick you in every which way. I hope I am not too spiteful in some of my questions. Think out of the box is my insightful suggestion. And if you get stuck, please don't you fear; the answer is always near.

> *"Don't be afraid to be confused. Try to remain permanently confused. Anything is possible."*
>
> George Saunders, *The Braindead Megaphone*

1. A black dog stands in the middle of an intersection in a town painted black. None of the streetlights are working due to a power failure caused by a storm. A car with two broken headlights drives towards the dog but turns in time to avoid hitting him. How could the driver have seen the dog in time?

2. A farmer in California owns a beautiful pear tree. He supplies the fruit to a nearby grocery store. The store owner has called the farmer to see how much fruit is available for him to purchase. The farmer knows that the main trunk has 24 branches. Each branch has exactly 12 boughs and each bough has exactly 6 twigs. Since each twig bears one piece of fruit, how many plums will the farmer be able to deliver?

3. What gets broken if it's not kept?

4. You can find it in Mercury, Earth, Mars, Jupiter and Saturn, but not in Venus or Neptune. What is it?

5. How far can a dog run *into* the woods?

6. What word is spelled wrong in every dictionary?

7. From a word of 5 letters, take 2 letters and have 1?

8. I'm in you,

   But not in him,

   I go up,

   But not down,

   I'm in the colosseum,

   But not a tower,

   I'm in a puzzle,

   But not a riddle.

9. Tommy Tucker took two strings and tied two turtles to two tall trees. How many T's in that?

10. What do you call a bear without an ear?

11. What letters express the most agreeable people in the world?

16. What word in the English Language is always spelled incorrectly?

12. What's a golfer's favourite letter?

13. Why is the letter A the most like a flower?

14. Why is the letter E like London?

15. I am in Time, and I am in Tie. I am in Fish, I am also sometimes only one. What Am I?

16. Which letter of the alphabet is very long?

17. Which letter of the alphabet is the silent member of the parliament?

18. Which letter of the alphabet wants to know the reasons all the time?

19. What is used to greet, and also used to describe something taller than you?

Fun and Funny Riddles

You can laugh; you can cry. You can think; you can sigh. You can get angry or happy, it doesn't matter to me. As long as you have fun and enjoy it, because that's what these riddles are for. If you like them then I promise there will be more.

"It's been my experience that you can nearly always enjoy things if you make up your mind firmly that you will."

Lucy Maud Montgomery, Anne of Green Gables

1. Why was the nose so tired?

2. Why did the turkey cross the road?

3. What type of music do rabbits listen to?

4. What did one wall say to the other wall?

5. Choose the correct sentence: "The yolk of the egg is white," or "The yolk of the egg are white"?

6. The more there is, the less you see. What is it?

7. What gets more wet while it dries?

8. Which month has 28 days?

9. Where do fish keep their money?

10. How did the soccer fan know before the game that the score would be 0-0? The score is always 0-0 before the game.

11. What snacks do you serve at a robot party?

12. Why don't cows have money?

13. What is it that never uses its teeth for eating purposes?

14. How did the chimp fix the leaky faucet?

15. What is the time-piece, that needs no winding?

16. If a red house is made of red bricks, and a yellow house is made of yellow bricks, what is a greenhouse made of?

17. What goes up but never comes back down?

18. You draw a line. Without touching it, how do you make it a longer line?

19. How can a leopard change its spots?

20. You bought me for dinner but never eat me. What am I?

Detective Riddles

Are you ready to be a detective? Here are some tricky riddles that require a little more thinking. Try and find the answers to all of these on your own, but if you just can't then the answers are shown.

"Oh the thinks you can think up if only you try!"

Dr. Seuss, Oh, the Thinks You Can Think!

1. Shauna was killed one Sunday morning. The police know who they are going to arrest from this bit of information:

   April was getting the mail

   Alyssa was doing laundry

   Reggie was cooking

   Mark was planting in the garden

   Who killed Shauna and how did the police know who to arrest?

2. Mr. and Mrs. Clyde went on a trip to the mountains. But 2 days later, Mr. Clyde returned home alone. He went to the police and said that Mrs. Clyde had fallen to her death.

The next day, Detective Stevens visited Mr. Clyde and arrested him for lying. Clyde confessed his guilt and asked the detective how he'd found out he was not telling the truth. Stevens said he'd simply called a travel agent and asked for some information.

What did the travel agent say to the detective?

3. Jack is placed in a cell with a dirt floor and only one window positioned so high no one could reach it. The cell is empty except for a shovel. It's dry and hot in there, but Jack won't get any food or drink

anytime soon. He has only 2 days to break out of the jail. If not — he'll die.

Digging a tunnel is not an option because it'll take more than 2 days. How should Jack escape the cell?

4. Mrs. Smith went to the police claiming that her vintage necklace was missing. When the police arrived, they saw no signs of a break-in. Only one window was broken. There was a total mess inside the house and dirty footprints all over the floor.

The next day, Mrs. Smith was arrested for fraud. Why?

5. Only one colour, but not one size,

Stuck at the bottom, yet easily flies.

Present in sun, but not in rain,

Doing no harm, and feeling no pain.

What is it?

6. Jack plays a sport and you need to find out what it is:

   Name the only sport in which the ball is always in possession of the team on defence, and the offensive team can score without touching the ball?

7. Is this true or false:

   A man can legally marry his widow's sister in the state of California?

8. It can't be seen, can't be felt, can't be heard and can't be smelt. It lies behind stars and under hills, and empty holes it fills. It comes first and follows after, ends life and kills laughter. What is it?

9. On the first day of the school year, all of the geography equipment was stolen. The police had 4 suspects: the gardener, the math teacher, the coach, and the school principal. They all had alibis:

   o *The gardener was cutting bushes.*
   o *The math teacher was holding a mid-year test.*
   o *The coach was playing basketball.*
   o *The principal was in his office*

The thief was arrested immediately. Who stole the geography equipment, and how did the police solve the mystery?

10. A serial killer kidnapped people and made them take 1 of 2 pills: one was harmless, and the other was poisonous. Whichever pill a victim took, the serial killer took the other one. The victim took their pill with water and died. The killer survived.

How did the killer always get the harmless pill?

11. Marissa and Juliana went out for drinks together. They ordered the same drink. Juliana was really thirsty and finished five in the time it took Marissa to finish one. The drinks were poisoned, but only Marissa died. How?

12. There is a priceless ornament found broken in a circular mansion. The detective interviews the cook, maid, and babysitter. The cook said he couldn't have done it because he was preparing

the meal. The maid said she couldn't have done it because she was dusting the corners. The babysitter said she couldn't because she was playing with the children. Who was lying?

13. A man went into a party and drank some of the punch. He then left early. Everyone at the party who drunk the punch subsequently died of poisoning. Why did the man not die?

14. Jack tells Jill, "This isn't the $5 bill you left on the table. I found it between pages 15 and 16 of Harry Potter."
Jill retorts, "You're lying and I can prove it."
How did Jill know?

15. A game set has gone missing from the classroom. Mr Robert called up 4 pupils and interviewed them. Only one of them is telling the truth.

These are the statements:

Alice: I did not take the game set.

David: I think Bob took the game set.

Bob: Alice is lying.

Carol: Bob is lying.

Who took the game set?

GNARLY RIDDLES

Love and Family

Welcome to level two of the riddles; here are some that will give you the giggles. Think about love, and family, and all things nice. Enjoy my love and family questions with a little more spice.

> *"There is nothing sweeter in this sad world*
> *Than the sound of someone you love*
> *calling your name."*
>
> *Kate DeCamilo, The Tale of Despereaux*

1. What relation would your father's sister's sister-in-law be to you?

2. A doctor and a boy were fishing. The boy was the doctor's son, but the doctor was not the boy's father. Who was the doctor?

3. Almost everyone needs it, asks for it, gives it, but almost nobody takes it. What is it?

4. Your dad was driving a black truck. His lights were not on. The moon was not out. A lady was crossing the street. How did the man see her?

5. I'm red, blood pumps through me, and I live in your body. I'm the symbol for love, please don't break me. What am I?

6. Please be patient, I'm new to the world. I cry a lot, please give me milk. Everyone smiles at me, please pick me up. What am I?

7. To some a source of trust and love,
   To others, ball and chain,
   For me some go beyond, above,

While others but complain.

For I'm a thing you cannot choose,

You're stuck with what you've got,

But I'm a thing that one can lose,

For granted, take me not.

8. With multiple colours, I appear after a storm. People like to point and take pictures of me. Some say if you look hard enough you will find gold on the other side of me. What am I?

9. Declaration of love

    Beginning of a journey

    With vows and a ceremony

10. I married your friend, I married your co-worker, I may have even married you, and I married every

girl that asks me to, yet I am still single. Who am I?

Animals and Things

Things that crawl are not my favourite, but I can't promise they won't be included. This is not too tricky and is rather fun if you ask me. Think like an animal and enjoy these riddles.

"The Rainbow Fish shared his scales left end right.
And the more he gave away, the more delighted
he became. When the water around him filled with
glimmering scales, he at last felt
at home among the other fish."

Marcus Pfister, The Rainbow Fish

1. Where can you find cities, towns, shops, and streets but no people?

2. A house of wood in a hidden place. Built without nails or glue. High above the earthen ground It holds pale gems of blue.

3. I am not alive, but I grow; I don't have lungs, but I need air; I don't have a mouth, but water kills me. What am I?

4. What goes up and down without moving?

5. What has to be broken before it can be used?

6. What building has the most stories?

7. I have a thousand needles but I do not sew. What am I?

8. What has wheels and flies, but it is not an aircraft?

9. No matter how little or how much you use me, you change me every month. What am I?

10. I run all around the pasture but never move. What am I?

11. A very pretty thing am I, fluttering in the pale-blue sky. Delicate, fragile on the wing, indeed I am a pretty thing. What am I?

12. What has a head and a tail but no body?

13. I weaken all men for hours each day.

    I show you strange visions while you are away.

    I take you by night, by day take you back,

    None suffer to have me, but do from my lack.

14. What kind of tree can you carry in your hand?

15. I come in many different colours and I get bigger when I'm full. I will float away if you don't tie me down and I will make a loud sound if I break. What am I?

16. What has hands, but is not flesh, bone or blood?

17. White and thin, red within, with a nail at the end. What is it?

18. What is black and white and is red all over?

19. The one who made it didn't want it. The one who bought it didn't need it. The one who used it never saw it. What is it?

20. What needs an answer but doesn't ask a question?

21. What two keys can't open any door?

Math Riddles

1 + 2 = 3 - I wish that is as simple as it could be. Math though, can get a little complicated; but I believe you are up for it. Figure out these mathematic problems or ask for some help.

"The only way to learn Mathematics
is to do Mathematics."

Paul Halmos

1. The ages of a father and son add up to 66. The father's age is the son's age reversed. How old could they be?

2. I am an odd number; take away a letter in the alphabet and I become even. What number am I?

3. I am a three-digit number. My second digit is 4 times bigger than the third digit. My first digit is 3 less than my second digit. Who am I?

4. You are given a telephone and asked to multiply all the numbers on the device's number pad. What will be the answer?

5. There are 100 pairs of dogs in a zoo. Two pairs of babies are born for every dog. Unfortunately, 23 of the dogs have not survived. How many dogs would be left in total?

6. How many sides does a circle have?

7. What do the numbers 11, 69, and 88 all have in common?

8. If four people can repair four bicycles in four hours, how many bicycles can eight people repair in eight hours?

9. It takes 12 men 12 hours to construct a wall. Then how long will it take for 6 men to complete the same wall?

10. Tom and Peter live in different parts of city but study at the same high school. Tom left for school 10 minutes before Peter, and they happened to meet at a park. At the time of their meeting, who was closer to the school?

11. Seven boys met each other in a party. Each of them shakes hands only once with each of the other boys. What is the total number of handshakes that took place?

12. When my dad was 31 years old, I was just 8 years. Now his age is twice as old as my age. What is my present age?

13. Suppose 8 monkeys take 8 minutes to eat 8 bananas. How many minutes would it take 3 monkeys to eat 3 bananas? How many monkeys would it take to eat 48 bananas in 48 minutes?

14. Find a 10-digit number where the first digit (most significant digit) indicates how many zeros are in the number, the second digit indicates how many 1s are in the number etc. till the tenth digit which indicates how many 9s are in the number.

15. A boy saw a shirt for $97 but does not have enough cash. So, he borrowed $50 from his mom and another $50 from his dad.
He bought the shirt, and got back $3 as change. He gave his dad $1 and his mom $1 and kept the other $1 for himself.

Now mom and dad paid $50 each and got back $1 each. So, they paid $49 each, totalling $98. The boy has another $1, adding up to $99. Where is the missing dollar?

Word Riddles

Big words and small words and all the words in between. This challenge requires you to think outside the box, but still think like an English Dean. Some are tricky and others are simpler than they seem.

"Anyone who can only think of one way to spell a word obviously lacks imagination."

Mark Twain

1. Jimmy's mother had three children. The first was called April, the second was called May. What was the name of the third child?

2. A truck driver is going opposite to the traffic on a one-way street. A police officer sees him but doesn't stop him. Why didn't the police officer stop him?

3. What is as light as a feather but the strongest man cannot hold for long?

4. What is always in front of you but can't be seen?

5. What building has the most stories?

6. There is a clerk at the butcher shop, he is five feet ten inches tall, and he wears size 13 sneakers. He has a wife and 2 kids. What does he weigh?

7. When may a man's coat pocket be empty, and yet have something in it?

8. I am the beginning of sorrow, and the end of sickness. You cannot express happiness without me, yet I am in the midst of crosses. I am always in

risk, yet never in danger. You may find me in the
sun, but I am never out of darkness.

What am I?

9. The more that there is of this, the less you see.
What is it?

10. It belongs to you, but other people use it more
than you do. What is it?

11. What can be big, white, dirty and wicked?

12. I weaken all men for hours each day.

I show you strange visions while you are away.

I take you by night, by day take you back,

None suffer to have me, but do from my lack.

13. You walk into a room with a match, a kerosene lamp, a candle, and a fireplace. Which do you light first?

14. A man was taking a walk outside when it started to rain. The man didn't have an umbrella, and he wasn't wearing a hat. His clothes got soaked, yet not a single hair on his head got wet. How could this happen?

15. Name four days of the week that start with the letter "T."

16. What word looks the same backwards and upside down?

17. A boy fell off a 20-foot ladder but did not get hurt. Why not?

18. How many letters are there in the alphabet?

19. You walk across a bridge and you see a boat full of people, yet there isn't a single person on board. How is that possible?

20. Which letter of the alphabet has the most water?

Fun and Funny Riddles

Time to laugh! Yes, these riddles aren't all funny – some are a little punny. Others are strange and unexpected, but that makes them exciting. You're only allowed to have fun during these riddles, no fighting.

"When fun gets deep enough

it can heal the world."

The Oaqui

1. Why do skeletons go on vacations alone?

2. What kind of music can you hear in space?

3. How do chiropractors swim laps?

4. Two girls were born to the same mother, at the same time, on the same day, in the same month

and in the same year and yet somehow, they're not twins. Why not?

5. A cowboy rode into town on Friday. He stayed in town for three days and rode back out on Friday. How is this possible?

6. I am a precious little thing, dancing and eating all the time. Watch me from a distance, so you can feel my warm and gentle love. But don't come to close or my next meal you could be!

7. The sun bakes them,
   The hand breaks them,
   The foot treads on them,
   And the mouth tastes them.
   What are they?

8. A precious stone, as clear as diamond.

   Seek it out whilst the sun is near the horizon.

   Though you can walk on water with its power,

   Try to keep it, and it'll vanish within an hour.

9. The rich men want it, the wise men know it, the

   poor all need it, the kind men show it.

10. Old McDonald owns me. What am I?

11. I spit a lot. You can get wool from me. What am I?

12. I work when I play and play when I work.

13. I look at you, you look at me

    I raise my right, you raise your left

    What is this object?

    It goes up and down the stairs without moving.

14. What can fill a room but takes up no space?

15. Who always enjoys poor health?

16. What do you call it when your parachute doesn't open?

17. Why did the pony cough?

18. What superhero is terrible at their job because they always get lost and are late?

19. What goes around and around the wood, but never goes into the wood?

20. How is Europe like a frying pan?

Detective Riddles

Okay Nancy Drew or member of the Secret Seven, now is time to look at some clues. No time to dilly dally, lives are at stake. See what is true and what is fake. So, put on your thinking caps and be very perceptive. I believe in you, detective.

"Nancy, every place you go, it seems as if mysteries just pile up one after another."

Carolyn Keene, The Message in the Hollow Oak

1. If a wheel has 64 spokes, how many spaces are there between the spokes?

2. Once on a winter day, John found his friend dead in his own house. John called the police and said that he was just passing by Jack's house and decided to come in.

He'd been knocking and ringing the bell for a long time, but all was silent. However, he could see the light in the room through a frozen window. He breathed on the iced window glass and saw Jack on the floor.

The police arrested John as the main suspect. Why?

3. A famous chemist was put to sleep in his own lab. There was no evidence except for a piece of paper with the names of chemical substances on it. On the day he was put to sleep, the chemist had only 3 visitors: his wife, Mary, his nephew Nicolas, and his friend Johnathan.

The police arrested the guilty suspect right away. How did they know who it was?

4. A man lights two candles and begins a romantic candlelight dinner with his wife. The candles are of equal length, but one candle is thicker than the other.

The thick candle is designed to last for 6 hours while the thin candle is designed to last for 3 hours.

At the end of the dinner, the thick candle is twice as long as the thin candle. How long did the dinner last?

5. A man started to town with a fox, a goose, and a sack of corn. He came to a stream which he had to cross in a tiny boat. He could only take one across at a time. He could not leave the fox alone with the goose or the goose alone with the corn. How did he get them all safely over the stream?

6. There was a man who was born before his father, killed his mother, and married his sister. Yet, there was nothing wrong with what he had done. Why?

7. What is the difference between a school boy studying and a farmer watching his cattle?

8. You are standing in front of a room with one lightbulb inside of it. You cannot see if it is on or off. Outside the room there are 3 switches in the off positions. You may turn the switches any way you want to. You stop turning the switches, enter the room and know which switch controls the lightbulb. How?

9. Suppose you want to send in the mail a valuable object to a friend. You have a box which is big

enough to hold the object. The box has a locking ring which is large enough to have a lock attached and you have several locks with keys. However, your friend does not have the key to any lock that you have. You cannot send the key in an unlocked box since it may be stolen or copied. How do you send the valuable object, locked, to your friend - so it may be opened by your friend?

10. I can connect you to the world but sometimes you ignore me. I'm covered with buttons and my sounds can be unique. Don't drop me or I might crack. What am I?

11. You are a junior detective investigating a case. Boys at an apartment complain that every day, they have an egg spinning competition with only raw eggs, and every day one particular boy wins.

The boys want you to find out how. You are observing the boy spinning an egg when suddenly it drops to the floor. The apartment clerk casually hands him a broom to clean it up, as if it happens every day. You now know why the boy always wins the daily competition. How?

12. I move very slowly at an imperceptible rate, although I take my time, I am never late. I accompany life, and survive past demise, I am viewed with esteem in many women's eyes.
What am I?

13. Some say we are red; some say we are green. Some play us, some spray us.
What are we?

14. A hunter met two shepherds, one of whom had three loaves and the other, five loaves. All the loaves were the same size. The three men agreed to share the eight loaves equally between them. After they had eaten, the hunter gave the shepherds eight bronze coins as payment for his meal. How should the two shepherds fairly divide this money?

15. A student zips on his scooter to ride to the train station to get to college. His home is close to two stops; the first one is a mile from home, and the second is two miles from home in the opposite direction. In the morning, he always gets on at the first stop and in the afternoon, he always gets off at the second one.
Why?

HELLISH RIDDLES

Okay ladies and gentlemen, now I'm bringing out the real riddles. Not that the ones before this weren't real, they were very real indeed. However, your brains are going to have to give it all you've got: the next riddles require take a little more thinking, whether you like it or not! I apologize profusely if after reading these then you no longer like me. Welcome to level three.

"Sometimes the questions are complicated, and the answers are simple."

-Dr Seuss

Love and Family

1. Three doctors said that Bill was their brother. Bill said he had no brothers. Who was lying?

2. I have ten or more daughters. I have less than ten daughters. I have at least one daughter. If only one

of these statements is true, how many daughters do I have?

3. Eros is at its core, while a ring is its symbol. Though it can be seen as holy, often it is sealed by contact. What is it?

4. This very thing you were born with pleases us all. It's even capable of making men fall, while only experienced by few it's treasured by all.

5. I am something quiet. I can be happiness, sadness or fear. I can show or just be gone, but I'll come back not before long.

6. Of no use to one, Yet absolute bliss to two. The small boy gets it for nothing. The young man has to lie or work for it.

The old man has to buy it.

The baby's right,

The lover's privilege,

The hypocrite's mask.

To the young girl, faith;

To the married woman, hope;

To the old maid, charity.

What am I?

7. Testimony of love

   Signifier of commitment

   All it needs is

   A bottle of wine

   And a band that shines

8. A mother has 5 children. Half of them are sons.

   Is this possible?

9. Who is bigger: Mr. Bigger, Mrs. Bigger, or their baby?

10. A mother has 6 girls and each of them has a brother. How many children are there?

Animals and Things

I hope you are not tired of animal riddles just yet. I have a few challenging ones for you to get. Some are about a wild animal, and some are about a pet. Some say you won't be able to find the answers, but I will never take that bet.

1. To cross the water I'm the way,
   For water I'm above; I touch it not, and truth to say, I neither swim nor move.
   What am I?

2. I have wings and I have a tail, across the sky is where I sail. Yet I have no eyes, ears or mouth, and I bob randomly from north to south. What am I?

3. I can fly, I can walk, and I can swim but I don't get wet. What am I?

4. What stinks when living and smells good when dead?

5. What is full of holes but still holds water?

6. When you have me, you feel like sharing me. But, if you do share me, you don't have me.
   What am I?

7. Turn us on our backs and open up our stomachs, and you will be the wisest but at the start a lummox.
   What are we?

8. What can run but never walks, has a mouth but never talks, has a head but never weeps, has a bed but never sleeps?

9. I am a box that holds keys without locks, yet my keys can unlock your deepest senses.
What am I?

10. What has one eye but cannot see?

11. It's been around for millions of years but is never more than a month old. What is it?

12. What tastes better than it smells?

13. What cannot talk but will always reply when spoken to?

14. I drive men mad for love of me, easily beaten, never free.

15. Pronounced as one letter;

and written with three,

Two letters there are,

And two only in me.

I'm double, I'm single,

I'm black blue and grey,

I'm read from both ends,

And the same either way.

16. What never asks questions but is often answered?

17. Come up and we go,

Go down and we stay.

18. What goes around the world without leaving its corner?

19. What word begins and ends with an E but only contains one letter?

20. What can run but can't walk?

Math Riddles

Now it's time to do some sums; test our brains and have some fun! Be careful though, these aren't always as they seem! Don't be scared; just give it a try. I promise it won't be 'do or die'...

1. Two fathers and two sons sat down to eat eggs for breakfast. They ate exactly three eggs; each person had an egg. Explain how?

2. There are a mix of red, green and blue balls in a bag. The total number of balls is 60. There are four times as many red balls as green balls and 6 more blue balls than green balls. How many balls of each colour are there?

3. A boy has as many sisters as brothers, but each sister has only half as many sisters as brothers.

How many brothers and sisters are there in the family?

4. When things go wrong, what can you always count on?

5. 16, 06, 68, 88, ?, 98

6. There are 2 ducks in front of 2 other ducks. There are 2 ducks behind 2 other ducks. There are 2 ducks beside 2 other ducks. How many ducks are there?

7. If there are four apples and you take away three, how many do you have?

8. Think of a number – any number! Add the number to the number itself and then multiply by 4.

Again, divide the number by 8 and you will get the same number once more. True or false?

9. I add five to nine, and get two. The answer is correct, but how?

10. Using only addition, how can you add eight 8's to get the number 1,000?

11. Raj has 2 books. One of the books is faced upside-down and the second book is rotated which makes the top of the book facing Raj. Then what will be the total sum of the 1st pages in each of these books?

12. I have a large money box, 10 inches wide and 5 inches tall. Roughly how many coins can I place in my empty money box?

13. Adored by few, feared and hated by many. Mistress of the entire universal reason, master in the art of numbers. Some may have solved many of your mysteries, but there still much of them to find.

    What are they?

14. A ship anchored in a port has a ladder which hangs over the side. The length of the ladder is 200cm, the distance between each rung in 20cm and the bottom rung touches the water. The tide rises at a rate of 10cm an hour. When will the water reach the fifth rung?

15. Matt is the fiftieth fastest and the fiftieth slowest runner in his school. Assuming no two runners are the same speed, how many runners are in Matt's school?

Word Riddles

Now it's time to get a little tricky with our words. Letters can get a little confusing at times, especially when it seems that everything rhymes. You take one out and put one in, and you have a new word with a completely different meaning: Bird turns to Bing; Bing turns to sing; sing turns to song… And this is taking too long. Please provide some help with punctuation and pronunciation problems that people prove to particularly need help with. Persevere and persist but remember to have peace and pleasure first.

1. What is the only English word, with two synonyms that are antonyms of each other?

2. A word I know, six letters it contains, remove one letter and 12 remains, what is it?

3. It happens once in a minute, twice in a week, and once in a year. What is it?

4. This five-letter word becomes shorter when you *add* two letters to it. What is the word?

5. What word has five letters but sounds like it only has one?

6. What begins with T, ends with T, and has T in it?

7. What question can you never answer yes to?

8. With thieves I consort, With the vilest, in short, I'm quite at ease in depravity; Yet all diviners use me, and savants can't lose me, For I am the centre of gravity!

   Hint: Read this one out loud.

9. In a one-story pink house, there was a pink person, a pink cat, a pink fish, a pink computer, a pink

chair, a pink table, a pink telephone, a pink shower – everything was pink! What colour were the stairs?

10. Forward and forward I go, never looking back. My limit no one knows, more of me do they lack. Like a river I do flow, and an eagle I fly. Now can you guess, what am I?

11. A girl is sitting in a house at night that has no lights on at all. There is no lamp, no candle, nothing. Yet she is reading. How?

12. If an electric train is going east at 60 miles an hour and there is a strong westerly wind, which way does the smoke from the train drift?

13. In the year 2000, a 40-year-old doctor told his son: "When I was a little boy, I decided to be a doctor

after seeing an internet website about performing a heart transplant on a puppy with a defective heart, so that the puppy would live a normal life." The son then thought that he would become a doctor so that I could help people in a similar way. What is the defect in this story?

14. Take away my first letter, then take away my second letter. Then take away the rest of my letters, yet I remain the same. What am I?

15. A murderer is condemned to death. He has to choose between three rooms. The first is full of raging fires, the second is full of assassins with loaded guns, and the third is full of lions that haven't eaten in 3 years.

     Which room is safest for him?

16. Dead on the field lie ten soldiers in white, felled by three eyes, black as night. What happened?

17. I have three syllables. Take away five letters, a male will remain. Take away four letters, a female will remain. Take away three letters, a great man will appear. The entire word shows you what Joan of Arc was.

18. Often talked of, never seen,
    Ever coming, never been,
    Daily looked for, never here,
    Still approaching, coming near.
    Thousands for its visit wait,
    But alas for their fate,
    Though they expect me to appear,
    They will never find me here.

19. I know a word of letters three, add two and less there will be.

20. We are such little tiny creatures;

   all of us have different features.

   One of us in glass is set;

   One of us you'll find in jet.

   Another you may see in tin,

   and the fourth is boxed within.

   If the fifth you should pursue,

   it can never fly from you.

   What are we?

Fun and Funny Riddles

These may be more of a challenge but they're also more fun. Find all the answers – whether it is an unexpected strange answer or a plain expected pun. Enjoy every minute of these, because soon my riddles will be all done.

1. Why did Momma Pig leave her husband?

2. What type of bean is a cannibal's favourite to eat?

3. What is the proper length for a lady's skirt?

4. You're driving a city bus. At the first stop, three women get on. At the second stop, one woman gets off and a man gets on. At the third stop, two children get on. The bus is blue and it's raining outside in December.

   What colour is the bus driver's hair?

5. There are three houses. One is red, one is blue and one is white. If the red house is to the left of the house in the middle, and the blue house is to the right of the house in the middle, where's the white house?

6. What starts out on four feet, then two in the and eventually three feet?

7. What travels faster: heat or cold?

8. Brothers and sisters I have, none but that man's father is my father's son. How could this be?

9. A box without hinges, a key, or a lid, yet golden treasure inside is hid.
   What is it?

10. As I walked along the path, I saw something with four fingers and one thumb, but it was not flesh, fish, bone or fowl.

11. I soar without wings; I see without eyes. I've travelled the universe to and fro. I've conquered the world, yet I've never been anywhere but home. Who am I?

12. Iron roof, glass walls
    Burns and burns
    And never falls.

13. Look at me. I can bring a smile to your face, A tear to your eye, Or even a thought to your mind. But I can't be seen.
    What am I?

14. I have keys but no locks. I have a space but no room. You can enter but can't go outside. What am I?

15. I can only live where there is light, but I die when the light shines on me...

16. What flies when its born, lies when its alive, and runs when its dead?

17. Every morning I am told what to do, and each morning I do what I am told. Yet I still can never escape your scold.

18. I am a mother and a father, but have never given birth. I'm rarely still but I never wander. What am I?

19. We hurt without moving; we poison without touching. We bear the truth and the lies. We are not to be judged by our size.

20. I'm always there, some distance away. Somewhere between land or sea and sky I lay. You may move towards me, yet distant I stay.

Detective Riddles

Look carefully at the clue, it is all up to you. A man lives; a man dies. Figure out the "who's", "what's" and "why's". Don't be scared, you are going to change the world. So, be brave and think smart, so you can find the solutions even when the truths have all been whirled and swirled.

1. Five children were playing kickball. One of the five broke a window. When questioned about the incident, each child made three statements of which two were true and one was false. The statements are given below.

Joe:

1. I didn't do it.

2. Sally will tell who did it.

3. One of us is in big trouble.

Matt:

1. Joyce did it.

2. I didn't do it.

3. I don't even like to play kickball.

Vince:

1. I didn't do it.

2. Joyce and I are good friends.

3. Sally doesn't know who did it.

Joyce:

1. Matt lied when he said I broke the window.

2. I never saw Vince before today.

3. I never broke a window in my life.

Sally:

1. I saw Joyce break it.

2. I didn't break the window.

3. I want to go home.

Who broke the window?

2. A prisoner is told: "If you tell a lie we will hang you, if you tell the truth we will behead you." What can he say to save himself?

3. If a boy blows 18 bubbles, then pops 6, eats 7 and then he pops 5 and blows 1.
    How many are left?

4. Your friend is in trouble, and she needs you to answer this riddle for her:
    If I am holding a bee, what do I have in my eye?

5. An old man dies, leaving behind two sons. In his will, he orders his sons to race with their horses, and the one with the slower horse will receive his inheritance. The two sons race against each other, but since they're both holding their horses back,

they go to a wise man and ask him what they should do. After that, the brothers race again — this time at full speed. What did the wise man tell them?

6. You are walking down a road and come to a fork. One path leads to certain death; the other leads to eternal happiness. You don't know which is which. In the middle of the fork, you come across two brothers who know which road is which. One brother always tells the truth and the other always lies. You can only ask them one question. How would you determine which road to take?

7. Four people arrive at a river with a narrow bridge that can only hold two people at a time. It's night-time and they have one torch that has to be used when crossing the bridge. Person A can cross the

bridge in one minute, B in two minutes, C in five minutes, and D in eight minutes. When two people cross the bridge together, they must move at the slower person's pace. Can they all get across the bridge in 15 minutes or less?

8. Turn me on my side and I am everything. Cut me in half and I am nothing. What am I?

9. After an accident, you are doing detective work on a crime scene when are asked this question: "Which tire doesn't move right when the car turns right?" What is the right answer?

10. One morning, little Mary got trapped in a castle in Costa Rica. There were 4 doors, but only one led to freedom. The doors opened up to the following:
    - Lava that would immediately melt anyone

- A killer clown that would beat any person to death
- A deadly frost that would freeze her at once
- Cops that would shoot any man or woman indiscriminately

Which door should she choose?

11. Guy de Maupassant hated the Eiffel Tower. So, every day, he had lunch in the one place where it couldn't be seen. What was that place?

12. Pete called his wife and said that he would be at home at 8. He came at 8:05. They had no special plans but still, the wife was angry because of his being late.

Why did she get so mad?

13. Brendon sat in the coffee shop and found a fly in his drink. He asked the waitress to bring him another coffee. After he'd received a new cup and taken a sip he got angry. Brendon realized that it was the same cup of coffee that he had in the first place.

How did he know he had the same cup of coffee?

14. John was alone at home and heard that something had fallen in his wife's room. He entered and saw that her favourite statuette was broken. At that moment someone ran out of the room. John tried to catch up with the stranger. But in the street the lenses on his eyeglasses fogged up because of cold weather. He could see nothing, giving the stranger the opportunity to disappear. John told this story to a policeman but he refused to investigate the

case. The cop asked him to stop lying and admit that it was he who had broken the statuette.

Was John's story actually fake?

15. Stan met a stranger whom he'd never seen before. Stan just heard about him and no descriptions of his appearance were ever mentioned. He wasn't famous. Nevertheless, Stan understood immediately who the guy was.

How was this possible?

RIDDLE SOLUTIONS

Cushy Riddles Solutions

Love and Family

1. Love.

2. Tulips

3. Tweet-hearts

4. All the couples survived.

5. Music

6. David!

7. Stick with me and we'll go places.

8. An apple a day keeps the doctor away.

9. Because love is blind.

10. The heart

Animal and Things

1. 3 flowers, 4 bees

2. A Turkey

3. By moving from one spot to another.

4. Penguin

5. Because you can see right through them.

6. It wasn't raining.

7. A Queen bee

8. Dog

9. Because they're stuffed.

10. Centipede

11. Stop imagining it.

12. You *quack* me up

13. Rooster

14. A *Tweet*ment

15. A gummy bear

16. A fly

17. A chick in its egg.

18. A sad zebra.

19. Hisss and Hersss

20. A chicken that plucks itself.

Math Riddles

1. Roosters don't lay eggs, silly!

2. Because seven ate nine.

3. He had 6 oranges to start with, and ate 2 the first day and 2 the second day.

4. She spent $7 on markers.

5. 4 children get 1 apple each while the fifth child gets the basket with the remaining apple still in it.

6. Only Tom was going to the park.

7. 9 (6+4=10; minus the one you've taken off the shelf)

8. Both these flights will be at the same distance from KL when they meet.

9. Eight – all the daughters share one brother.

10. None of the hens are now remaining (27-5=22; 22-13=9; 9-9=0)

11. Two hens are needed.

12. One and a half hours is the same as 90 minutes.

13. The bottle costs $1.05 and the cork costs 5¢.

14. You will need to buy:

    a. 19 Chicken eggs cost 95 cents

    b. 1 Duck egg cost 1 cent

    c. 80 Goose eggs cost 4 cents

    Total of 100 eggs (19 + 1 + 80 = 100) for 100 cents (95 + 1 + 4 = 100).

15. His sister is 99 years old. When Tom was 2 years old, his sister was 1 year old. 98 years later, he becomes 100 years old. And 98 years later, his sister will be 99 (98 + 1) years old.

16. Number of cookies:

    a. Twelve

    b. Twelve

Word Riddles

1. I didn't say anything about night-time! This was happening during the day.
2. None – it is a pear tree so it does not produce plums.
3. A promise
4. The letter "r".
5. Halfway. Once it reaches halfway, it's running out of the woods.
6. Wrong
7. Alone
8. The letter "u".
9. There are two T's in "that".
10. The letter "g".
11. A "b".
12. "U" and "I"
13. Incorrectly
14. Tee
15. Because the B is after it.

16. Because E is the capital of England

17. The Letter I. The letter I is in every word it is in "I am in tIme, and I am in tIe, I am in fIsh," The letter I can also be alone in A Sentence. Example: Well, I can be alone!

18. The letter "Q"

19. The letter "I". "I" is not pronounced when we say "parliament".

20. The letter "Y".

21. Hi

Funny Riddles

1. It was running all day.

2. To prove he wasn't chicken!

3. Hip-Hop

4. "I'll meet you at the corner."

5. Neither! The yolk of an egg is yellow, not white.

6. Fog

7. Towel

8. All of them.

9. In a riverbank

10. The score is always 0-0 before a game.

11. Assorted nuts.

12. Because the farmers milk them dry.

13. A comb

14. With a monkey wrench.

15. He sipped his coffee before it was cool.

16. A rooster

17. Glass, all greenhouses are made of glass.

18. Your age

19. Draw a short line next to it and now it's the longer line.

20. By moving from one spot to another.

21. Cutlery

Detective Riddles

1. April killed Shauna because there is no mail delivery on Sundays.

2. The travel agent said, "Mr Clyde had bought two plane tickets to the destination and only one return ticket."

3. Jack should use the shovel to make a pile of dirt under the window, climb on it, and escape from his cell.

4. The police were sure that Mrs. Smith lied to them because the window was broken from the inside. If it was broken from the outside, little pieces of glass would be on the room's floor.

5. Shadow

6. Baseball

7. False, the man is dead if she is a widow.

8. The dark

9. The thief was the math teacher. According to his words, he was holding a mid-year test, but the crime happened on the first day of the school year.

10. Both of the pills were harmless. The poison was in the glass of water the victim drank.

11. The poison was in the ice. Since Marissa's ice had time to melt, she was poisoned but Juliana wasn't.

12. The maid. There are no corners in a circular mansion.

13. The poison from the punch came from the ice cubes. When the man drank the punch, the ice was fully frozen. Gradually, as the ice cubes melted the poison was released into the punch.

14. Harry Potter, like all other books, has odd-numbered pages on the right. Therefore, pages 15 and 16 are the front and back of a single page, and nothing could have been found between them.

15. Alice took the game set and Bob is telling the truth.

Gnarly Riddles Solutions

Love and Family

1. This person would be your mother

2. His mother.

3. Advice

4. It was a bright, sunny day.

5. Your heart.

6. A baby

7. Family

8. Rainbow

9. Marriage

10. The priest

Animals and Things

1. A map

2. A nest

3. A fire

4. Stairs

5. An egg

6. A Porcupine

7. A garbage truck

8. Calendar

9. The fence

10. A butterfly

11. A coin

12. A window

13. A palm

14. A balloon

15. Clock

16. Finger

17. Newspaper

18. Coffin

19. A telephone

20. A monkey and a donkey

Math Riddles

1. There are three possible solutions for this: the father-son duo could be 51 and 15 years old, 42 and 24 years old or 60 and 06 years old.

2. Seven (Take away "s" and it becomes "even")

3. 141

4. Zero. The keypad on a calculator contains a 0, and anything multiplied by 0 is 0.

5. 977 dogs (100 x 2 = 200; 200 + 800 = 1000; 1000 – 23 = 977).

6. Two – the inside and the outside.

7. They all read the same upside down.

8. 16 bicycles

9. No time! There is no need of constructing it again as the job is already done.

10. They are both at the same distance from school as they met in the same place.

11. 21

12. When you calculate the difference between the ages, you can see that it is 23 years. So, you must be 23 years old now.

13. If 8 monkeys take 8 minutes to eat 8 bananas, then 1 monkey takes 8 minutes to eat 1 banana. 3 monkeys will take 8 minutes to eat 3 bananas.

    1 monkey can eat 1 banana in 8 minutes, so 1 monkey can eat 6 bananas in 48 (8 x 6) minutes. Therefore, 8 monkeys can eat 48 bananas in 48 minutes.

14. 6210001000

15. Let's see what happens to that $100. The shirt costs $97, the boy keeps $1 and mom and dad get $1 back. That adds up fine.

    Now let's look at the second way. How much money did they end up paying? Well $98 dollars, and $97 of it went for the shirt and $1 to the boy. Now, that adds up too.

The problem with the question is that the $1 that the boy keeps is contained in the $98 that they end up paying so we shouldn't expect them to add to anything meaningful.

Word Riddles

1. Jimmy
2. The truck driver was walking on the side of the road; not driving.
3. Breath
4. The future
5. The library
6. He weighs meat.
7. When the pocket has a hole in it.
8. The letter "s"

9. Darkness

10. Your name

11. A lie

12. Sleep

13. The match.

14. The man was bald.

15. Tuesday, Thursday, today and tomorrow.

16. SWIMS

17. He fell off the bottom step.

18. Eleven: T-H-E-A-L-P-H-A-B-E-T.

19. All the people on the boat are married.

20. The letter "C".

Fun and Funny Riddles

1. Because they have no body to go with.

2. A nep-tune

3. They do back stroke

4. Because there was a third girl, which makes them triplets!

5. His horses name was Friday.

6. Fire

7. Grapes

8. Ice

9. Love

10. A farm

11. A llama

12. A musician

13. Mirror

14. Carpet

15. Light

16. The doctor

17. Jumping to conclusions.

18. He was a little horse.

19. Wander woman

20. The bark on a tree.

Detective Riddles

1. 64. The space that comes after the 64th spoke, would be just before the first spoke.

2. John wouldn't be able to unfreeze the window glass because it's usually icy on the inside.

3. The piece of paper had a clue on it. If you combine the short names of the chemical substances on the paper, you'll get a name: Ni-C-O-La-S.

4. The dinner lasted 2 hours.

   In 2 hours, the thick candle was 2/3 of the original length and the thin candle was 1/3 of the original length.

5. He took the goose over first and came back. Then, he took the fox across and brought the goose back. Next, he took the corn over. He came back alone and took the goose.

6. His father was in front of him when he was born, therefore he was born before him. His mother died while giving birth to him. Finally, he grew up to be a minister and married his sister at her ceremony.

7. One is stocking his mind, while the other is minding his stock.

8. You turn 2 switches "on" and leave 1 switch "off" and wait about a minute. Then enter the room, but just before you enter, turn one switch from "on" to "off". Once in the room, feel the lightbulb - if it is warm, but off, it has to be the last switch you turned off. If it is on, it has to be the switch left on. If it is cold and is off, it has to be the switch you left in the off position.

9. Send the box with a lock attached and locked. Your friend attaches his or her own lock and sends the box back to you. You remove your lock and send it

back to your friend. Your friend may then remove the lock she or he put on and open the box.

10. A Cell Phone

11. The clerk handed the boy a broom, so the egg the boy was spinning must have been hard-boiled.

12. I am your hair.

13. Pepper

14. The shepherd who had three loaves should get one coin and the shepherd who had five loaves should get seven coins. If there were eight loaves and three men, each man ate two and two-thirds loaves. So the first shepherd gave the hunter one-third of a loaf and the second shepherd gave the hunter two and one-third loaves. The shepherd who gave one-third of a loaf should get one coin and the one who gave seven-thirds of a loaf should get seven coins.

15. The stations and his home are on a hill, which allows him to ride down easily on his scooter.

Hellish Riddles Solutions

Love and Family

1. No-one is lying; the three doctors are Bill's sisters.

2. If I have any daughters, there will always be two statements which are true. Therefore, I have no daughters.

3. Marriage

4. Your beauty

5. Feelings

6. A kiss

7. Proposal

8. Yes. I didn't say the other half weren't boys...

9. The baby, because he is a little Bigger.

10. 7 – each girl has the same brother.

Animals and Things

1. A bridge

2. A kite

3. A bird's shadow

4. Bacon

5. A sponge

6. A secret

7. Books

8. A river

9. A piano

10. A needle

11. The moon

12. Your tongue

13. An echo

14. Gold

15. Eye

16. A doorbell

17. Anchor

18. Stamp

19. An envelope

20. A drop of water

Math Riddles

1. One of the 'fathers' is also a grandfather. Therefore, the other father is both a son and a father to the grandson. In other words, the one father is both a son and a father.

2. Number of balls:
   a. Blue balls = 15
   b. Red balls = 36
   c. Green balls = 9

3. Four brothers; three sisters

4. Your fingers

5. The "?" is the number 78 - all the numbers read 86 through to 91 when read upside down.

6. Four ducks, sitting in a square formation

7. You took three apples, so you obviously have three.

8. True.

9. I am working with time: you add five hours to 9am, and get 2pm.

10. 888 + 88 + 8 + 8 + 8 = 1000

11. 2. Regardless of how the books are oriented, the first page of every book is page number 1. So therefore, 1 + 1 = 2!

12. Just one coin; after that it will no longer be empty.

13. Mathematics.

14. The tide raises both the water and the boat so the water will never reach the fifth rung.

15. There are 99 runners in Matt's school.

This is tricky. If Matt is the fiftieth fastest runner, he would be number 50 in the sequence 1, 2, 3...50. To be the fiftieth slowest, he'd have to be number 50 in the sequence 50, 51, 52...99, since there are fifty numbers from 50 to 99 inclusive.

Word Riddles

1. Cleave

2. Dozens

3. The letter "e"

4. Short.

5. Queue

6. A teapot

7. Are you asleep yet?

8. The letter "v"

9. It is a one-story house, so there are no stairs.

10. Time

11. The woman is blind and she is reading Braille.

12. It is an electric train so there is no smoke.

13. The internet did not exist yet when the father was a young boy.

14. The postman

15. The third room – lions who haven't eaten in three years are now dead.

16. A bowling ball knocked down ten pins.

17. Heroine

18. Tomorrow

19. Few

20. The vowels - a, e, I, o, u.

Fun and Funny Riddles

1. Because he was a boar.

2. A human-being

3. A little above two feet.

4. Whatever colour *your* hair is, since you're driving the bus.

5. In Washington D.C.

6. A human being – a baby crawls on all fours; then we learn to walk on two feet; and eventually when we get old, we walk on three feet (two feet and a crane or walking stick).

7. Heat travels faster because you can catch a cold.

8. You are looking at yourself in the mirror.

9. An egg

10. A glove

11. Imagination

12. Lantern

13. Memories

14. A keyboard

15. A shadow

16. Snow flake

17. An alarm clock

18. Tree

19. Words

20. The horizon

Detective Riddles

1. Vince did it.

Joyce's statements 1 and 3 must be true. If she had broken the window, both statements would have been false. But since each child told only one lie, these two statements must be true. Therefore, Joyce's statement 2 is the one that is false.

The statement of all the other children can then be proven true or false using this information.

Since we know that Joyce's statement 2 is false, Sally's statement 1 and Matt's statement 1 have to be false. Joe's statement 2 has to be false, since Sally did not tell who did it. Now we are left only with Vince.

2. Nothing

3. One

4. This riddle is a play on the proverb, "Beauty is in the eye of the beholder." In this case, you are the "bee-holder." Thus, beauty is in your eye.

5. After they switch horses, whoever wins the race will get the inheritance because they still technically own the losing (i.e., slower) horse.

6. Let's say the path on the right leads to eternal happiness. After you ask your question, both brothers will tell you the exact same thing: "He would say the left path leads to eternal happiness." In either case you would pick the opposite of what they both say, because one is telling the truth about it being a lie, and one is lying about it being the truth.

7. The group of four must follow these steps.

- First, A and B cross the bridge and A brings the light back. This takes 3 minutes.
- Next, C and D cross and B brings the light back. This takes another 10 minutes.
- Finally, A and B cross again. This takes another 2 minutes.

8. The number 8. The number 8 looks like an infinity symbol if it's turned sideways. Cut in half, the digit looks like two zeros.

9. The spare tire.

10. The cops would shoot any man or woman, but Mary isn't an adult.

11. He ate in the restaurant that was located at the base of the tower.

12. Pete should have come at 8 p.m., but he came home at 8:05 a.m. the next day.

13. "The second" coffee was sweet already. Brendon had put sugar in his "first" cup before finding the fly.

14. Yes, it was. John ran out into the street while chasing a stranger. But eyeglass lenses don't fog up when a person comes out of a warm room and into the cold. He was just afraid to confess to his wife that he had broken her favourite statuette.

15. He was a twin brother of one of Stan's friends.

Made in the USA
Coppell, TX
01 April 2020